821

Give
Yourself
a Hug

Grace Nichols

Illustrated by Kim Harley

PUFFIN BOOKS

For Lesley, Darren and dear little Marcus –
keep on hugging

PUFFIN BOOKS

Published by the Penguin Group
Penguin Books Ltd, 27 Wrights Lane, London W8 5TZ, England
Penguin Books USA Inc., 375 Hudson Street, New York, New York 10014, USA
Penguin Books Australia Ltd, Ringwood, Victoria, Australia
Penguin Books Canada Ltd, 10 Alcorn Avenue, Toronto, Ontario, Canada M4V 3B2
Penguin Books (NZ) Ltd, 182–190 Wairau Road, Auckland 10, New Zealand

Penguin Books Ltd, Registered Offices: Harmondsworth, Middlesex, England

First published by A & C Black (Publishers) Ltd 1994
Published in Puffin Books 1996
3 5 7 9 10 8 6 4 2

Text copyright © Grace Nichols, 1994
Illustrations copyright © Kim Harley, 1994
All rights reserved

The moral right of the author has been asserted

Filmset in Palatino

Made and printed in England by Clays Ltd, St Ives plc

Except in the United States of America, this book is sold
subject to the condition that it shall not, by way of trade or otherwise,
be lent, re-sold, hired out, or otherwise circulated without the publisher's
prior consent in any form of binding or cover other than that in which it is
published and without a similar condition including this condition being
imposed on the subsequent purchaser

Contents

Morning

Morning comes
    with a milk-float jiggling

Morning comes
    with a milkman whistling

Morning comes
    with empties clinking

Morning comes
    with alarm-clock ringing

Morning comes
    with toaster popping

Morning comes
    with letters dropping

Morning comes
    with kettle singing

Morning comes
    with me just listening.

Morning comes to drag me out of bed
    — Boss-Woman Morning.

Sun Is Laughing

This morning she got up
on the happy side of bed,
pulled back the grey sky-curtains
and poked her head
through the blue window
of heaven,
her yellow laughter
spilling over,
falling broad across the grass,
brightening the washing on the line,
giving more shine
to the back of a ladybug
and buttering up all the world.

Then, without any warning,
as if she was suddenly bored,
or just got sulky
because she could hear no one
giving praise
to her shining ways,
Sun slammed the sky-window close
plunging the whole world
into greyness once more.

O Sun, moody one,
how can we live
without the holiday of your face?

Feeling Hungry

When you're feeling hungry
time can go by so slowly,
like when I'm out shopping
with me Mum.

I say, 'I'm hungry'
She says, 'You've just eaten'

I say again, 'But I'm still hungry'
She says again, 'But you've just eaten'

'Well I don't know, it must be the cold,
but me belly feel like a doughnut with a hole.'

Me And Mister Polite

Again and again
we met in the lane.

We met in the sunshine
We met in the rain
We met in the windy
We met in the hail
We met in the misty
And autumn-leaf trail
On harsh days and dark days
On days mild and clear

And if it was raining
He'd say, 'Nice weather for ducks'
And if it was sunny
He'd say, 'Good enough for beach-wear'
And if it was windy
He'd say, 'We could do without that wind'
And if it was nippy
He'd say, 'Nippy today'
And if it was cold-windy-rainy-grey
(which it nearly always was)
He'd say, 'Horrible day'
Or 'Not as good as it was yesterday'

And he'd hurry away with a brief tip of his hat
His rude dog pulling him this way and that.

First Spring

You know that winter's almost gone
when you step outside and feel
the first warm fingers of the sun
touching your back,
like a hesitant friend.

You know that winter's almost gone
when you walk around
and suddenly, in the back garden –
a posse of daffodils
nodding to the earth's sweet hum.

Now, you're running out the gate
Now you're running . . . down the pave
There's a shout in your wave
There's a skip in your sing.

It's the first day of spring.

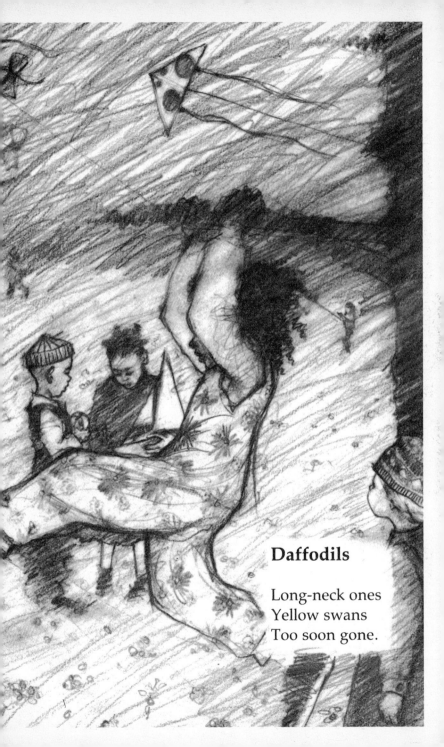

Daffodils

Long-neck ones
Yellow swans
Too soon gone.

For Dilberta
Biggest of the elephants at London Zoo

The walking-whale
of the Earth kingdom – Dilberta.

The one whose waist
your arms won't get around – Dilberta.

The mammoth one whose weight
you pray, won't knock you to the ground.

The one who displays toes
like archway windows,
bringing the pads of her feet down
like giant paperweights
to keep the earth from shifting about.

Dilberta, rippling as she ambles under
the wrinkled tarpaulin of her skin,
casually throwing the arm of her nose,
saying, 'Go on, have a stroke'.

But sometimes, in her mind's eye,
Dilberta gets this idea – She could be a Moth!
Yes, with the wind stirring behind her ears,
she could really fly.

Rising above the boundaries of the paddock,
Making for the dark light of the forest –

Hearing, O once more, the trumpets roar.

Roller-Skaters

Flying by
on the winged-wheels
of their heels

Two teenage earthbirds
zig-zagging
down the street

Rising
unfeathered –
in sudden air-leap

Defying law
death and gravity
as they do a wheely

Landing back
in the smooth swoop
of youth

And faces gaping
gawking, impressed
and unimpressed

Only mother watches – heartbeat in her mouth

My Gran Visits England

My Gran was a Caribbean lady
As Caribbean as could be
She came across to visit us
In Shoreham by the sea.

She'd hardly put her suitcase down
when she began a digging spree
Out in the back garden
To see what she could see

And she found:
That the ground was as groundy
The the frogs were as froggy
That the earthworms were as worthy

That the weeds were as weedy
That the seeds were as seedy
That the bees were as busy
as those back home

And she paused from her digging
And she wondered
And she looked at her spade
And she pondered

Then she stood by a rose
As a slug passed by her toes
And she called to my Dad
as she struck pose after pose,

'Boy, come and take my photo – the place cold,
But wherever there's God's earth, I'm at home.'

When My Friend Anita Runs

When my friend Anita runs
she runs straight into the headalong –
legs flashing over grass, daises, mounds.

When my friend Anita runs
she sticks out her chest like an Olympic
champion – face all serious concentration.

And you'll never catch her looking around,
until she flies into the invisible tape
that says, she's won.

Then she turns to give me
this big grin and hug

O to be able to run like Anita,
                    run like Anita,
Who runs like a cheetah.
If only, just for once, I could beat her.

Listening To My Big Sister's Denim Rave

'Nothing to wear
but Mum don't care.
You'd think to lend me
her new leggings
was a crime –
Hey, what's this
at the bottom
of the clothes-pile?

My old shelter-in-a-storm,
my fashion-saviour
the number in which
I can't go wrong.

No matter the fray
No matter the rip
No matter the stain
No matter the split
with a bit of lipstick
could even look chic.

Well, watch me
slip/zip/trip
in my old denims
watch me
slide/stride/glide
in my old denims
watch me
dance/prance/as I advance

Well, who can stop me
in my old glad-mads?
Who can stop me when
I take my street-cred stance?'

In With The Rhythm

In with the rhythm
In with the swing
In with the mood
Of the laser-lightning

> Music the finder
> of cord on my brain
> Music the magic that takes
> away my homework-strain
> Music the maker that makes
> all movement come unchained

In with the rhythm
In with the swing
In with the mood
Of the laser-lightning

Turn up the music
And close the door
Hip-hop time
On my bedroom floor

'Summer Is Hearts' Says Sammy Selvon

skies bluer
larks truer

sun golder
folks bolder

leaves lusher
bees buzzer

grass deeper
fruit sweeter

'Summer is hearts' says Sammy Selvon,
munching his slice of water melon.

Berries

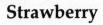

Strawberry

You wear your heart
on the edges
of your green sleeves,
hanging small and red,
close to the fields,
Strawberry –
studded with tiny seeds
of love.

Blackberry

Velvet pouch
of sweetness
this is true –
We have to prick hands
to get you.

Raspberry

It's the rasp
in your berry
that makes us tick.

It's the tang
in the flavour
that gives us a kick.

But raspberry
why does one of
your tiny pulps – all aglow

Remind me so
of a full-blooded
mosquito?

Mister Goodacre's Garden

The neighbours say he's weird and wicked
Just cause Mister Goodacre won't mow down
His high grass or thicket,
(Their own lawns look ready
for billiards or cricket)

I guess he just loves tall grass waving
I think the length of his dandelions amazing,
But the neighbours keep throwing him these
spearing-looks,
Which seem to say, 'You're lowering the tenor
Of the neighbourhood.'

Mister Goodacre just stands there
Whistling carefree,
Waving a water-gun for all to see;
'Think me lazy,' he says, 'think me crazy,
But I will defend my dandelions and daisies'.

More power to your wild flowers, Mister Goodacre,
But while you're basking . . .
I'm afraid the neighbours
Are planning a grass-murder
With their lawn-mowers.

Counting Sleep

I've tried counting sheep
even goats that bleat and frogs that leap
I've tried falling slow-motion into the ocean
and counting the fish in the deep

But I can't seem to slip into sleep
I've tried both the heavenly and earthly approach
cloud-counting star-counting grass-counting
pebble-counting
I've even tried counting with humming:
> *'Ten green bottles standing on the wall*
> *Ten green bottles . . .'*
But no, I don't accidentally fall
with the green ones in a heap

At last – I give up in defeat
I just know I'll never slip into s
s
s
z
z
l
l
l
e
e
e
p

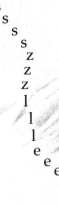

In The Great Womb-Moon

In the great womb-moon
I once did swoon

Time was a millennium
In my mother's belly

There was water
There was tree
There was land
There was me

Time was a millennium
In my mother's belly

There was planet
There was star
There was light
There was dark

Time was a millennium
In my mother's belly

How I frog-kicked
And I frolicked
Like a cosmic
Little comic . . .

Then came a century, the waters subsided,
I was forced out like a morning-star
Into the borders of another world.
I'm not unhappy, but sometimes,
There's a wee mourn in me for the time when –

Time was a millennium
In my mother's belly

31

Carnival-Time

'Look how they coming, Mummy,
Big-storm down the street,
Look how they coming like palm trees
Come to wave in London, Mummy,
The music itching me feet
The music itching me feet

Look how they moving, Mummy,
Movements-wicked in the street,
Look how they jumping and bouncing,
Like rhythm come to shake-up brick houses,
Mummy,
The music itching me feet
The music itching me feet

Look how they flowing, Mummy,
River-rippling down the street,
Look how they flowing like a boat-of-music,
come to glide on the Thames, Mummy,
The music itching me feet
The music itching me feet

Look at Bearman and Beastman bouncing,
Mummy,
Look at the Dragon-Lady,
Look at small boy flouncing, Mummy,
Look . . .'

'Boy, No-way, No-way,
you full of poetry,
but you ain't jumping in no band today,
not until you finish that homework – Hear what I say.'

Tube-Trapped

Tube-trapped
Tube-trapped
Boy, I'm
Tube-trapped

Can't move forward
Can't move back
Mustn't get
A panic-attack

And the minutes
Ticking by –
Slow and thick
As jelly

Wish I'd taken
Time to put
Some breakfast
In my belly

Tube-trapped
Tube-trapped
Guess I'm really
Tube-trapped

Can't move forward
Can't move back
Just a sardine
In a pack

What if I snap?
And today's the day
Mom's forgotten to slip
An apple in my rucksack.

Sea-Rock

Sea rock us to love
        rock us to love

Breeze glad us to touch
        glad us to touch

Sun shift us in strides
        shift us in strides

Trees keep the gold and green of memory
        keep the gold and green of memory

But most of all sea
        rock us to love
        rock us to love

Autumn Song

Rusty-red, yellow,
Brown
Summer's gone,
Winter to come

By the windfall of apples
And the stripping of trees
By the pick-up of conkers
And the carpet of leaves

By the tired-face flowers
And the mould on the mound
By the soles crunching berries
And the bees' farewell-hum

Rusty-red, yellow,
Brown
Summer's gone,
Winter to come

Tree-Money

Autumn
is tree-money
everywhere on the ground –
red, gold, brown.

39

Gull

The oil-stricken gull
has struggled ashore,
and although full-grown,
looks like a bewildered
scraggy fledgling.

Her oil-tarred wings
seem heavy as lead
as she totters slightly,
stiff-legged.

Staring out at us
with an unblinking
atomic,
almost comic surprise.

She hasn't taken any sides
but she's lost her natural home
and more. An unanswerable cry
is stuck in her throat
                    Why?
                        Why?
                            Why?

The Dissatisfied Poem

I'm a dissatisfied poem
      I really am
there's so many things
      I don't understand
like why I'm lying
      on this flat white page
when there's so much to do
      in the world out there
But sometimes when I catch a glimpse
      of the world outside
it makes my blood curl
      it makes me want to stay inside
and hide
      please turn me quick
before I cry
      they would hate it if I wet the pages

The Day They Turned The Clock Back

The day they turned the clock back
I nearly got a heart-attack

It looked so cold
It looked so dark

I knew my mother would say,
'No park'

I knew I couldn't stay out late,
Like summer when I stayed out till eight.

Snowflake

Little shaving
of hot white cold
Snowflake
Snowflake
you really bold

How you feeling, Snowflake?
Icily-Hot
How you feeling, Snowflake?
Ice-Silly-Hot

Snowflake
Snowflake
you little clown

    c
     a
      r
      n
     i
     v
      a
      l
       l
        i
       n
      g

        d
         o
        w
         n

A small ghost kiss
on my warm tongue.

Making My First Snowman In My Mother's Pink Rubber Gloves

I scooped and shaped him lovingly,
I piled and patted best as could be,
though my pink hands were burning me,
I kept on building my first snowman.

I shaped his shoulders and fixed his neck,
I smooth his face and rounded his head,
though my pink hands were freezing me,
I kept on building my first snowman.

I put the usual carrot in, for the nose,
a banana for a mouth, my two best conkers for
his eyes,
though my pink hands were killing me,
I kept on building my first snowman.

I threw my Dad's black jacket
to keep the cold from his back,
I stuck on his head the old felt hat,
then I stepped back.

Why was he staring at me with those big eyes?
Why was he so freezingly alive?
Man, why was he looking at me so?
Oh, No,

He wasn't a snowman.
HE WAS A SNOWCROW!

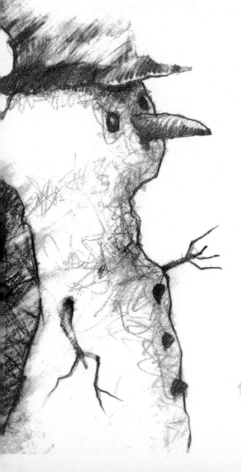

Stormman

He snatches up
all the little winds
growing big
under the hood of his skin.

He bays at the skies
bringing down thunder
and lightning
on his side.

He works himself up
into a hunger-sucking rage.
With his whirring-eye
and his hurricane-style

With his flapping-fling
and that singeing-sting,
who can stop him
as he comes howling in?

A man werewolf
size like King Kong
so, Stormman comes
whittling down.

Picking up the waves he's raised
he bashes the sea-front,
throwing himself about further inland;
battering windows and doors;

Clawing up rooftiles;
and heaven help anything not secure
like dustbin covers!
Stormman just sends them flying like frisbees.

Getting up
in the middle of the night,
I reach to put on the light.
Suddenly –

Stormman knocks out Electricity,
sending me stumbling
back to bed
as if from a Bogey

By morning
all worn-out
a limp thing –
he crawls out back to sea.

But look at the debris.
Look at the countless fallen trees.
The harvest of shambles,
Signing his name everywhere –

StormMan Waz Ere

Hail Me!

Suddenly I came –
little ice bullets instead of rain

I ping-ponged
on the rooftops
I spin-spun
in the gutters
I bounced down
on the concrete
I hit upon
the flowers
I rolled off
the edges
of window-ledges
and hedges

I lay around
for as long as I could
(which in my case was only five minutes)
then I vanished.

Weather-Moan

How it kyan snow so
How it kyan cold so
How it kyan fog so
How it kyan frost so
How it kyan rain so
How it kyan hail so
How it kyan damp so
How it kyan dark so

Is how it hard so?

Spell To Bring Out Back The Sun

Banana of my life
Golden-delicious of my eye

Crisp in the crunch
Jewel in the crown

Flounder in the sea
The beesknee – the beesknee

Sun, come out and play
your yellow symphony.

Grown-Up Parties

I love having parties
but not my Mum
as soon as the invitations have gone
she begins to look glum

Fretting, regretting,
pacing up and down
my Dad cannot placate her
as she mutters in a frown:

'Elizabeth – a carnivore
Henry – allergic to cheese
Valerie – a calorie-counter
Mira – gluten free
Percival – now vegan
Susan – she can sense if it's organic
And I must remember last time
the non-meaters got non-roast, I mean nut-roast,
. . . no, this time I mustn't panic.'

And on the day of the party
it's always the same confusion –
Dad chopping up the onions
tears streaming down his cheeks,
Mum blending up the nut-roast
and sprucing up the leeks,
Dad just misses chopping off his finger
as Mum moodily repeats:

'Elizabeth – a carnivore
Henry – allergic to cheese
Valerie – a calorie-counter
Mira – gluten free
Percival – now vegan
Susan – she can sense if it's organic
And I must remember last time
the non-meaters got nut-roast . . .
Now who picked up the garlic?'

Grown-up parties!
Why can't she just give dem –
Crisps and ice-cream and smarties?

Dream-Lady

Old-Lady, Dream-Lady
carrying your home around
in a supermarket trolley

Pushing it lopsided
right down the middle
of the traffic

Like an own-way crab
on wheels,
trying to steer it clear,

Horns honk
heads peer
but Old-Lady, Dream-Lady
gives it all an indifferent stare

She's heading
for the big furniture store.
She's heading to set up home
Soon as the doors are closed –

To wrap herself once more
in her cardboard world of dreams.

Listening To A Tale About A Mum And Dad

Dad has given up smoking.
Mum has not.
They quarrel a lot.

Every time Mum lights up a fag
Dad throws open the window
As if to get rid of a fog.

'You're polluting the place,' he says.
Mum gives him a glare,
And goes on puffing like an engine anyway.

Then Dad who's lost his job says,
'You'll die of lung cancer,'
'Like hell I will,' Mum puffs back in answer.

I sit through it
As though I'm dumb
What will become of Dad and Mum?

Give Yourself A Hug

Give yourself a hug
when you feel unloved

Give yourself a hug
when people put on airs
to make you feel a bug

Give yourself a hug
when everyone seems to give you
a cold-shoulder shrug

Give yourself a hug –
a big big hug

And keep on singing,
'Only one in a million like me
Only one in a million-billion-thrillion-zillion
like me.'

Index Of First Lines